T0051404

SOMETHING, I FORGET

Angela Leighton was born in Wakefield, educated in Edinburgh and Oxford, and has taught at the universities of Hull and Cambridge. The daughter of a Yorkshire (composer) father and a Neapolitan mother, she has always recognised her heritage of mixed languages and conflicting standpoints. Her book, *Hearing Things: The Work of Sound in Literature* (2018), sets autobiographical prose beside critical writing to suggest the connections between them, while her volume, *Spills* (2016), interweaves memoir, short story and translation with original poetry.

She has published poetry and short stories in many magazines, including the *New Yorker*, *TLS*, *Poetry Chicago*, *Archipelago*, *The Dark Horse* and *PNR*. This is her sixth volume of poetry.

ALSO BY ANGELA LEIGHTON

Poetry

One, Two (Carcanet, 2021)

Spills (Carcanet, 2016)

The Messages (Shoestring, 2012)

Sea Level (Shoestring, 2007)

A Cold Spell (Shoestring, 2000)

Critical

Walter de la Mare: Critical Appraisals (ed with Kajita, Nickerson) (Liverpool, 2022)

Hearing Things: The Work of Sound in Literature (Harvard, 2018)

Voyages over Voices: Critical Essays on Anne Stevenson (ed) (Liverpool, 2010)

On Form: Poetry, Aestheticism, and the Legacy of a Word (Oxford, 2007)

Victorian Women Poets: A Critical Anthology (ed with Reynolds) (Blackwells, 1995)

Victorian Women Poets: Writing Against the Heart (Virginia, 1992; 2019)

Elizabeth Barrett Browning (Harvester, 1986)

Shelley and the Sublime (Cambridge, 1984; 2013)

Something, I Forget

ANGELA LEIGHTON

CARCANET POETRY

First published in Great Britain in 2023 by
Carcanet
Alliance House, 30 Cross Street
Manchester, M 2 7 A Q
www.carcanet.co.uk

ISBN 978 1 80017 353 8

Book design by Andrew Latimer, Carcanet
Typesetting by LiteBook Prepress Services
Printed in Great Britain by SRP Ltd, Exeter, Devon

The publisher acknowledges financial
assistance from Arts Council England.

CONTENTS

STONE GROUND

SEA CROSSINGS

RIDDLING HELL

SUMMONING HEAVEN

REMEMBERING GARDENS

I made this. I have forgotten
And remember.

T. S. ELIOT

A poem will be written if in the grip of memory
we are able to forget.

JAMES LONGENBACH

A thought in your ear, my friend – a word in your pocket.

A phrase for fingering, player – a tune for caressing.

A breath in your hair, love – a touch of nothing.

A line in your sight, reader – a space for pausing.

A beat in your leaving, traveller – a time for going.

A verse in your hand, my dear – to keep… forgetting.

SOMETHING, I FORGET

STONE GROUND

Grief cuts no ice.
Its stone drives deep.

It sings to keep
a silence live.

It laughs to cry.
Then takes the long

steep road – to write
a way to weep

SNOWDROP

I dropped off just now and dreamt I was writing to you –
and maybe I was, or am – tenses confuse.
So we'll take what comes in the present, whether dreamed or no,
use handy pronouns – *I*, most like this wand
of a pen that wavers along the line's narrow feint –
a perfect blank of thought or paper, verse
or purpose – for the feints of phrase we might call true.
For I was never just mine, or you, you.

Something I wanted to say which slips my mind…
So here's a garden instead, and a snowdrop stiffened –
its natural antifreeze anticipating zero
(survival technique), like unfeeling learned, like frozen
bedrock closeting its secret deep in the earth.
Here's my wilding garden of remembrance. It will run
to seed. But today, deep winter clamps and leaves
just a fragile whiteness surprised in its shivering bracket.

FROST WORK

Jack-the-lad with his spray-can whitener
gifts a cruel jewelry to the world:

sparkling moonstones for the bones of branches
prickly karst to stiffen the short grass

flecks of pearl for the crossbeam webs
opals to frill the wings of cyclamen,

and a frozen kiss for that alabaster look-alike:
Cupid with a bird-bath, poised to draw

an arrow across quartz water, cracked
for thirst, for love – for solvencies of rain.

WATER LIKE A STONE

Christmas, a cold day –
and lost to ourselves in a windless heaven
with all that story fallen away
(peace and goodwill, a baby in the hay)
we walk uphill from the world's quarrelling,

our company, weather –
true cosmopolitan fetched from elsewhere,
drifter-stranger – and we together
following the night's sketchy snow for a trail
to the late moon's uplands, one step away,

reach a small shore –
water polished to a drumskin of ice
where each skimmed stone knocks for a door
to leave, but skips, teasing with repeats,
its note multiplying birds of nowhere.

It's as if you heard
creation's chip skidding high and clear
over glacial wastes, and imagined a bird –
one, then another – voiced from sound waves,
shivered from the physics of touch and air.

My one last throw…
a stone to try this basin of iced rain,
the tarn's soundboard struck accelerando
to scatter, for luck, a kerfuffle of bird notes –
and win a love song from the earth's deep cold.

SKATERS

Too hard   this earth   to download   the dead
speed   the soul's   equivocal   committal.

These flood plains'   levels   lie sheer and silver
though a minus-10   wind-chill   stone-cold weather

chisels dry air   saps   and prises
each visible breath   knives an icing

where something   leggy or winged   comes to life
on the flooded fen's   reflecting outlook

its glassy   logbook   recording   long slides.
Like dancing ephemera   waving to drown

racing to founder   they suddenly   stop short
pausing   then fall   or else   take a wide

cursive   swipe   freestyle   that might
carry   a bodyweight   on dangerous ground.

Wide loops   turn-abouts   writing for life
they hop   spin   no stopping   glissing

a criss-cross   (listen)   till something underground
beneath the icesheet   shifts   and a crack

whipcracks   under axel   death spiral   under self's
slicing   signature.   Tomorrow,   ice-melt.

PEBBLES

Sea's worry beads
        breves, vocables snapped in stone
like o's and oh's
        their cuddled hard-hearts rolled in cold.

Glossed by waves
        to rose or grey, amended by millennia
they rattle on the drag
        that cracks no code, but only realigns

(like words for pain)
        their coasting turnover, shiftless lie.

STONE PRAYER

Give us this earth that deeps to rock yet keeps its temperate crust that stops
the light the air the living from heat that is the magma's fiery inner
cauldron of a heart that needs no beat but is what sparks this airy bowled
planet at the start.

Give us this stone no carbon-dating calibrates that knows no change
but goes before bacterial mats conceived of us and stores the star that
holds the fire that flared its sign and formed us in earth's elementary
crucible of stuff.

Give us this time just one split-fraction of all the aeons that cooled and set
in solid stone from four thousand million years ago and will outlive
the breath the bread the breaking nano-seconds of us who waste in time
to grist and silt.

Give us this world that turns in space to make the time we must compute
by day or night by heart or clock by breath or step by tick tock till
tripped up on sedimentary rock that grinds to soil and feeds the wheat
that takes the sun

to make the bread our bones grow from till thinned and fallen bone to stone
like twinned offspring timed and rhymed like lifelong longing to lie down
we home in this hard ground and give the mineral gift of ourselves again to
earth as it is

earth as it is.

TARN AND WALL

I set out in sun to reach that shore –
    the climb's surprise
among the higher fells – its wide-open eye
    a bowl of ice-melt
brimful, sky-struck, a cup for the gods.
    But found instead
this Damascene stop – a blindness sudden
    as the unread rock

of a sheltering wall topped with slate –
    each upright blade
a transverse fipple to the wind's ways
    each hearting-stone
a keeping lock to baffle the rain's
    crosswise slam
and a driven pashm of mist everywhere
    infilling the visible

where all I find is a coating of star-moss
    galaxies of green
the tiny life's clinging resilience
    and a dry-stone wall's
soaked reserves of stony minerals –
    my one gain to be
crouched to the coldest thing – like a tomb –
    learning to see.

VILLA DEI MISTERI, POMPEII

In the city of the dead
a redstart startles the stonework, flirts and flares
　with tail feathers spread,

then chips, chips –
(a mason chiselling a stone – whose name is it?)
　A dead leaf flips

where a lizard darts
and a shiver rakes wild mint like something passing.
　What is it starts

to unsettle the still
noonday heat earthed deep in this stony place,
　packed with its kill,

its clinker, cavities?
A small child squats and sorts random igneous rocks
　ignoring all this

happy in the dust
to heap up mock-volcanoes from the mountain's cast-offs.
　How something lost

and purposeless
(like that one fresco'd shoe no one answers to –
　mysterious address

to someone slipped
just out of the picture, was it moments or millennia ago?
　or maybe just tripped

away, leaving stones
a child collects to pen the terrors of the world) –
   still ghosts what remains.

   A bird's chip grades
the silence, incised. Far off, I imagine a footstep
   clips, and fades.

One of the villa's mysterious frescoes shows a single, apparently
unattached shoe.

So who, forgetting,
just hopped away, or dropped it, maybe? from bike or backpack
on a winter fenland path that rides
the nearly imaginable curve of the earth?

Larger than life –
from a distance maybe the bloom of a flower? – (litter, more like) –
but it's only a whitish trainer thrown
by-the-by, off-course, shiny in microfibre.

Someone should bin it,
tidy the land that's green and level for miles around.
But no, its lostness stands to attention,
a step, but no sound, an open question.

What size? Whose fit?
Something rootless haunts about its shape, its look of missing,
pointless yet pivotal, ordinary, surprised.
A spoor of laces tangles on the ground.

It might be a sign –
a thing never finished, only abandoned – like half a rhyme.
It stays faithful to being forgotten,
points the way like a lostness found.

Days later, no change –
its hollow, too human, exposed to the sky, mouthing its secret
like no one's business, voice crying for a cry.
Here's hoping, it dreams – *hoping*, a small ask.

ON THE COBBLED WAYS

Sampietrini (so quaint a name,
pet-saint or santon of Rome's old ways?) –

these little St Peters, quilts of cold,
whisper *Quo vadis?* from each cobbled stone.

Uneven floors of the city's story,
fathomable squares, ghost-goings, inroads –

they fan in circles, make a calculable maze
to save us knowing what lies below:

shards, shells, middens, skulls,
the crumbled calcium of the antique dead.

A mechanical digger now frets their bedding
for a drain, gas mains, pipework for the living.

And still I go rooting in chinks and grooves
among corks, crown caps, cigarette butts, coins

for what might fall in the way of things,
adding its own deposit of dross

to shore up centuries of lives to come
in miniature tenements of memory and loss.

*

Sampietrini, then – to find them out
I play the child's old stepping game,

foot-to-foot where the generations fled
signing their weight on each cool tab –

shady floaters, shying familiars,
dodging us every step we take,

but one among them with younger face –
is it you in your time, I in mine,

in a cross-rhythm that aparts our lives?
The city's loveliness still sings a love song

to dream, to pass on… stones pave the way.
These basalt wedges grip their underground.

Think *Morra*, our fate, that ancient game:
no flesh cuts stone, no stone weathers rain.

So step on step I walk to their tread
and leave the light imagination of a print,

a mute impress, a caress in the wind –
no hint but love that we came, and went.

FOR A ROMAN SHADE

and find a way into a city I keep trying
to near-miss.

Stav Poleg, 'Drawing Lesson: Rome'

1 LAPIS NIGER

Writing's a near-miss, nearer or further, however you go
about to find the charm in a pit, the curse on a stone:
'Who violates this spot be banished to the spirits of the underworld'.
Lapis Niger – an ox-plough script like hooves in a furrow
and a black marble slab to cover the restless stories below:
foundling tales of the meadows, a shepherd, twins and a wolf.

Or: *A narrow lane, an old man, and two boys.* I think
Posthumus, returned to life from his old Roman ground.
So foundlings might found a city, a nation, an empire, a story
and stories muddle like roots stirring the humus to life,
cropping through stones and tombs: mallow, toadflax, fumitory,
capers trailing the travertine, campion seeding the roadside.

The city's unquiet, sleeping pastoral takes them to heart,
as it takes the night-time scribes, the spray-can minstrels who come
from Tiburtina, Cinecittà, to fable the old walls
with love-pierced hearts, rude cock-and-balls, lyrical one-liners –
where something still biding its time must tap, and tap…
What lies beneath the founding stone? – what lies beneath that?

Lapis Niger – the black stone lying over the supposed grave of Romulus, the
legendary founder of Rome, which bears this curse.
Posthumus – a character in Shakespeare's *Cymbeline*, which also tells of two
foundling boys harboured by a country shepherd.

2 Stone Pine

Is it the droughts of summer twist them awry?
    stunt their uprightness
like the arrested cry of something pining
    inside? –

bearing their heavy headgear, turned from us
    like wavering dotted i's
scribbled in time, crooked, each one
    against sky.

A child might trace the perfect spiral of a cone,
    shuttered so tight no finger
could prise a nut from those close-lipped, wooden
    mouths.

But once he found in the shade of our loved tree
    a prize, free for the picking:
a cone, wide open as an advent calendar,
    promising

its sweets, fallen lightweight, lucky at his feet.
    But all he held was a grimy
empty rattle – first grit, then a scared black bug
    dropped from it.

3 Dis Manibus

Why then, year after year, return?
to find what I crave and miss each time
gathering like spirits in a crowded place –
Dis Manibus packed beneath –

jostling to catch an eye, a hearing,
to lean their starved dead empty heads
towards a thought, a phrase – to snatch
from scraps of wording memories of themselves:

the known, unnamed, the loved, the strange,
the lost in time or found too late –
and that one boy who crossed to join
the joyless playgrounds of the underworld.

His shade might bite on a word for lifeline,
turn from eternity's stony quiet
to feel the rhythm of a remembered rhyme:
Who's there? Who's there? Knock for no answer.

We knew he'd not outlive that summer.
Lost friend, here's a line, a verse that comes
as near to saying: I'd send any word
to feed your hunger, jog a heartbeat.

Dis Manibus – the shades of the underworld. Letters found on
innumerable commemorative tablets and graves.

4 LIBATION

How thoughtlessly we assign them heaven,
commend them beyond the sky's blue yonder
     to everlasting bliss.

     Might they not miss
our changeable ways and fitful habits?
the light's alterations on this suffering planet?

But we shut them up in everlastingness,
barricade the view, close the border.
     Maybe they'd rather

     we left an aperture
to ease the passage of their nothingness
back to the half-light haunts of our brains?

That day I spilled a little red wine
by mistake, laughing, and watched it drain
     in the shade of a pine,

     making a beeline
for memories buried long decades ago.
So I tunnelled a thumb-hole, and planted a small cone.

5 Marble Boy

The anonymous sculptor had done his best
to soften a marble box to a bed
with rolled headrest, an impression of cushions,

with mock-folds hung to-the-life, floor-length.
Such comforts the artist artfully gave
to see him through, to last the night –

but still the boy looks wakeful, unconvinced,
propped fully dressed, not wanting to sleep yet,
as if not quite taken in by the game,

whatever it is, being played against him.
One hand lies slack beside rattle or top,
the other, cupped to his ear, only makes

his look more listening, faraway,
as if he could hear other days, other shores,
struck by a thought in the stone of his brain.

Too young, too real, he stares wide-eyed –
no fool to sleep so early in the day,
his look too wise, as if to say:

I see through your game, your early-to-bed,
your art's fine trick that is the marble's gain.
But give me my life, my life, again.

I touch that hand to know how coolly
carved, how perfect, unheld, quite alone –
and think: what will survive of us is stone.

A PARTING STONE

Write less, I told myself. So how much is that?
More-or-less, a voice replied – and duly tossed
a scrambled alphabet into that whirling roulette.

How long have I got? I persisted. Why the long and the short's
as far as it goes, from here to there, from cone
to seed, seed to cone, till suddenly it's over.

How reckon the way? Take a walk, it said. Here's grit
over granite, shale over slate, and the wind in a wainstone.
It sings strange notes. Cut – to a whetstone finish.

SEA CROSSINGS

Across this rockery of terracotta
these roof-tiles braiding like a tress of waves
where tenuous aerials net their calls
and a gull's wing tests highways of air

I hear above the city's hubbub
miles of ocean messaging elsewhere
space and leaving, salt and weathering
the open waters in the cup of my ear.

RAIN FUGUE

A chivvying rain
tills and frets
this open shoreline's
crumbly ways
where a sad boy waits
to play, please play.

But a humdrum downer
dragging swags
of duck down cloud
throws pins of wet
(like acupuncture
percussing the levels)

and pricks this grave
of kibbled shellfish
milled silica
old fossil bits
of graptolitic
shale or slate.

The boy stands still.
Rain's a runaway.
It draws a veil
(oh lachrymosa)
and puckers the sand's
flat-packed grains.

Fugitive rain
you'll take the sea-road
run soft to salt
and seep belowground.
That boy must weep
for the day's lost play.

RAIN SCHERZO

Plink like:	tinny pips
tinkering	piccolo
small blips	tippytoes
drop-ping	drop-ping
pingo	a brimful
tipples	tiddlywinks.
Plink like:	plectrum
plethora	or plural
pluvial	imploring
nib-bling	nib-bling
to whittle	stone ground
to watery	beginnings.

SEA LEVEL

Exhausted – in sleep so deep it trawls
a depth of still, to feel for the sea's

push and leave, hush and slither,
the slack of a thing inching to take

sticks, stones, shell, weed,
and braille the sand beneath each wave

like the last touch of a blind man's hand
reading a page of the earth's lost ground.

                    *

For here's the fault-line of an old contention:
sea draws, withdraws, a creature steeped

in itself, no hurry, and heaves like breathing –
then spills, and leaves its secrets torn

to pieces, cut-work bridalling the rocks,
and falls, collapses, stiffening to froth

as the drag sings and circles, winning
its dream of us, returned to beginning.

THE ROAD TAKEN: LARPOOL VIADUCT
(i.m. N. H.)

Finally to here:

        this high brick giant's striding edge

so many feet above

        the slatted, dovetailed shale that flakes

to blades in your hand.

        Once these rails brought the children back

year in, year out.

        Now only ghost trains ride the cinder track

time's night-trippers.

        Will they take me with them? as they took the child

excited, frightened

        by a drop too sheer below the window

and only the sea's

        distant level to steady the terror.

*

Finally to here:

                    this red-brick shelf stepped across a gap

fettled at base

                    an industrial wind-harp played by changing

crossroads of weather.

                    I might stand dreaming forever on this height

open to nowhere

                    lovelier than this, this earth in space

embraced by sky

                    counting the moments of a life come home –

its stations of the way

                    and a long road taken, north – south – north,

to reach this full sum:

                    the viaduct's airy viaticum.

SEA FRET

Attento si fermò com'uom ch'ascolta:
ché l'occhio nol potea menare a lunga,
per l'aere nero e per la nebbia folta.

Dante

A scope of falling underlies our height –
where boulder clay goes sheer to scree
or tacked by roots of gorse and thorn

and sea writes reams of easy verse –
an epic set in moveable type
between blue distance and infinity,

and we are lords of our own little day –
a short forever like heaven at hand
and earth an edge to ground us high

above the fulmars' flight display –
above the grief that's writ on water
like lives forgotten, or given for lost —

                    *

till warm air thickens, the distance creeps
nearer as sea gives up its ghost
to finger along this ledge of rock

like all our shades amassed from dream
crowding to steal the air we breathe,
bluffing the sea-view, impeding the way

where we stand close and lost as they
in a ghost-cumulus contingently adrift,
coasting the route of an unfenced path

now shrunk to a lyke-wake pass, a step
no wider than this: *see,* mere standing room
beside a fall, cliff-edge for inching,

and self our only given, soon missing.

IN A GLASS, LIGHTLY
(from the Venetian Islands)

My dear, I think neither rule nor spell
can wish them back, the nameless, the lost.
Here I walk in the city of water
and learn the art of pausing, to know

how carnival in a mask comes home
with ashen beak and goggle eyes –
old crow in a domino – summoning those
who must play their part in the bone-pit's casino.

For here are places, forgotten cremations –
plague, smallpox, cholera, covid –
where high brick walls still hide what's below
though water seeps and salt winds corrode,

and tides rearrange a necklace of weeds
on dead-end steps given to reflection,
and abandoned islands quarantine their dead
where wild flowers mark what no one remembers.

*

Yet here's liquefaction of sand and silica –
the clotted miracle of a red-hot spit
fired in the heart-lock, tipped for quickwork,
turning its molten ball to a bauble

that lives by a thread of breath, inspired –
a thing so shatteringly fine it cries
aloud in its skin, makes light of nothing,
and shapes a solid as clear as day:

a snake, a stallion, cut-glass ephemerids,
a moth so fragile, so invisibly visible
it's as if you milked the sky to make
a spirit come by, breathed on, soufflé.

Now see, it's won like a crystal soul
from grit and flame, like the ghost of a smile.
Consider – don't touch! – in a glass, lightly,
creation's toy unbroken for a while.

WESTWARDS FROM VENICE

Petrochemicals –
spires of steel, chimneys, calligraphies
nibbing the horizon.

A sky in manacles –
shackled highlights of a day darkening
glitter of poison.

A filigree of quills
hard-wiring the sunset's merciful halo
for diesel, kerosene.

A tall flame spills
to warm our skins, speed our living.
Original sin.

FOR A GLASS HARP

A loom of crosswires, cranes on the lagoon.
Horizons of islands, the index of a tower.
A gull, pitch-perfect on a tripod of groynes,
quills registering winds and tides.

Low wastes of marsh, samphire and glasswort.
An egret stepping coolly to the edge.
Narcissus observed in the meniscus of a pool.
The city dreams of itself, and reflects.

Arabesques of marble over sump and drain.
Salt waves crumbling the brick's feet of clay.
Virgil's finger points one way. *Quick.*
Crackpot reflections make crazy paving.

                    *

Then a girl stops me dead – for a tune, divining.
Sifter, sommelier, she brushes the lip
of each glass spirit's calling echo
and stirs a resonance, conjures up

oh love, my long-lost, my many forgotten.
In a dead-end alley I hear what might sound
as she touches each cup, to raise by numbers
the song's loveliness, fingering its round.

And somewhere I hear them, voiced and passed,
belled in each glass more caressed than struck –
it chambers an echo, catches the last…
and makes a note to save what drowns.

FISH MARKET

Packed box of loot
                    silverware from the smith of the sea
movie of fins and gills and tails
                    sync-swimming you'd think
yet still and mute,
                    their look a scream our ears never hear.

Bream and bass and amberjack
                    with diamanté
gleaming backs
                    and small fry tossed like silver pieces
where a bleary swordfish points to accuse
                    heaven of murder.

Only the live
                    lumbering clubfoot of a lobster feels
for sea's deep wavering caress
                    in a glass tank of weed
baffled to reach
                    through plastic leaves' everlasting green

the end of its world, so close and soon.
                    Our reckoning, this
this, our disaster
                    guilt, and art. How profligate
our need to live, yet wit to grieve
                    the things we kill.

FROM THE LIGHTHOUSE
(for Anne Stevenson)

Far-seeing stroke, oblivious blessing –
its smudged gold riffs a slow thumb-roll
over the sea's darkening skin.

It might be death's old news, recalled
across the night's irresolvable distances
bringing you round and round on earth –

aerialled here, where this beam of light
repeats its measure, shines, yet keeps
brushing aside, aside, aside

the dark's starlit, moth-eaten curtain,
the cursive restlessness of waves
that hide the enigma of what lies deeper –

while news love meant to keep forever
is wiped, so lightly, by this scanning weeper.

FROM POETRY'S LIGHTHOUSE, AGAIN

Lonely inside.
Here's one last stand
in the art of stopping.
An edge, a lookout.
It might be a lifelong
practise for the end.

So pause, rock-fast.
Friend, are you here
where a Fresnel lens
is turning its head?
Send news. Send word.
Maybe lend an ear?

Sea air's a seasoning
too salt for green.
Yet seablite, purslane,
glasswort survive
the waves' rock-a-bye,
the storm's careen.

We've been here, remember?
Each high white tower
an edgy groundling
set to deliver
illuminations
by rote, by the hour,

by pause and beat
(oh distractions clarify)
by swipe and repeat.
Self's frail composite
attends what must come.
Each pulse is I.

On sand, waves scribble
their memoir for the day.
The tides' massif
in motion replies:
Erase. Erase.
Then you went away.

This signal station
searchlights the sky,
gives ear to otherwise.
Who's to say
this night's too dark?
My dear, goodbye.

SOUND CROSSINGS

Thole's an oarlock	to steady each bend.
To thole's a lament	when the road's at an end.
Paddle has no thole	to help steer the way.
To paddle's like footsie	sea-stepping, child's play.
Lap's like a last	you might have to take.
Sea laps onshore	not a drink to slake.
Slake is a mudflat	shined by the tide.
To slake proves thirst.	What proves you died?
Die's what was cast	life's line for the port.
To die's the last meta-	phor: trans-port.

LAUNCHED

A wish as Odyssean, as old as time,
drives this child's one toy of a thousand ships:

a rickety craft of sticks in binder-twine,
a white-rag sail to twitch on an offshore wind.

From a stubby pin of cane a mast aspires.
The knotted joins are frayed, the flat hull gapes.

Millennia before the wheel, a log was launched
when some brave human mounted a dream to leave –

just so this primitive mock-up bobs and turns,
bounced on the waves' small hobbles, rocked and trialled

like a saint's coracle trusted to weather and luck,
yet carried by some momentum the spirit craves.

                    *

It rides one level slack, then rafts a rhythm
that *will* play catch-up, but now only taps … taps

as the ocean's covert incalculable pulse upholds
this tacky throwaway, ropey panpipe of twigs.

Then one wave risen out of sync just swivels the thing
and it surfs, backed up by the roll, to an easy landing.

A slake of mudflats shines in the noonday sun.
Wet sand, raked by a tide, displays what must come.

But the child, driven by hope, and passion, and faith,
wades deeper in to speed her wish, test-launch

her self's way out from safe and steadying ground
to a space (at heart) as wide and free as the world.

BY THE TIDE OF HUMBER

(In 1641 Andrew Marvell's father was drowned cross-
ing the Humber in a barrow boat. The poet's 'To his Coy
Mistress' was written some nine years later.)

Which way to walk? – eastwards by ebbtide,
past the stink of the upriver staiths
and a small brick school between garden and church,
to the spit of Spurn, that land's-end shifter,

or westwards inland, the estuary shrinking
till you'd almost walk across sandbanks and mud
southwards to Cambridge – the way out, straight
by Ermine Street for a Roman departure.

Now *I by the tide of Humber* once more
ponder these shallows more lethal than deeps,
and a barrow boat, grounded, where a wash of water
unpicks what was lost of him bit by bit –

and think, no *fine and private place*
was his, just the city's effluent waste
seeping seawards, the spirit of him held
forever in the tide's endless erasures,

till Spurn divides sea-lippers from the still
to curb the hackling flow that pours
salt into fresh, daily, and seems
a hurt refreshed, a trouble restored.

Now I, by the tide, still whisper farewells.
Te patre, Caesar (royal head or round?) –
my warring self by such waters crossed:
fluvial, marine, knitting frets between

where contrary currents make shifting sands,
channel a rip-tide, then swing and suck
any light craft under – as if I carry
his death within, unfinished, unsung.

So I, by the waters that quarrel and kill,
stay, for contraries no war resolves,
to complain of love in verse that hides
an elegy, deep in the undertow of *tide*.

'*Te patre, Caesar*' – 'you father, Caesar', from Marvell's earliest
known student poem in Latin, published in Cambridge, 1637.
Other words in italics from 'To his Coy Mistress'.

SONNET FOR A FISHERMAN
(after another capsizing, Sicily)

Now he's turned his back on the sea,
     its livings, killings,
Pasquale docks a fleet of miniatures
     high-and-dry --
each plywood strip cambered, sealed,
     glossed ship-shape
to take the mountain ranges of the waves
     heaved in its way
like any stormy dream that sweeps
     his sleeping brain.

Long days he sits in an airless room
     to flitch and chip
the wood's life-saving way of being
     hollowed, prowed --
though each float sits on a cross of sticks
     unmoved, mid-air.

Now he's done with fishing, Pasquale
     nets no catch
except what a trawl of memory throws up:
     (don't look, don't touch,
the roll will take it out, disperse
     its pieces of a life.)
So he chisels another – will it ferry the load
     of souls who'd go
safe as houses for a home this night?
     But his craft's too light.
It keeps the finish of an art that knows
     no human cargo.

ELEGY: LONG CROSSINGS

Full moon's in love with water, and leaves a sign:
this crazing face spilt on a moving base,

like a spectral reminiscence slipped out of mind.
Such lunacy, to love black water so,

to fall for it, then stay and ride the waves
like a paper doily floated, or a lotus flower.

Black mirror, stressed and whorled, obsidian sea
on which the moon's medusa, flailing, seems

a plasm of light that makes nowhere more clear –
white heart of darkness, pulsing, holding fast

against the rush and passing – phantom token
stayed, like something breaking, never broken.

                    *

So dream might net oblivion's deeps and find
someone, I forget – friend of a short night fled,

fellow of almost never, long lost to me.
So memory's darkening book retains no face.

What's this, then, pooled in the waves' amnesiac tug?
apparencies of moonshine, paramours,

one luminous dogged light riding beside
as we buck small waves and leave a wake behind.

Here's something known at removes, yet close as touch,
like love for one who left without a name

and went far out, far out – now suddenly found
late surfacing with all life's faces drowned.

*

Small graves attend this walking on the sand.
Low shallows take what comes and must go on,

so crumbling landfill fills the print I leave,
swallows the space shoes dent, leadweights my feet.

You feel it, how your spring is sucked back in.
Quicksteps are how you keep from slip and drowning,

tucking each shoe in grainy spills to lift,
as grit compresses and all your boneweight goes

forward again, free from that burying stay,
heel and toe caressing sand's underlay.

*

So weather's laid like letters, s's, f's –
a ripple rhythm scored onshore, as if

the graphics of a storm, imprints of wind
had signed their wavelengths lengthwise on the sand.

I might be tracing mega-tons of fall
in these light scriptures waving out of line,

or tracking drifts from miles or months ago
that scribble memorabilia where they land –

like travellers making notes, or poets knowing
the lag of what's forgotten is fillip for going.

DITTY FOR THE POETS

For *hornlight* (Hopkins) – moon's gold-sound in sight.
For *slughorn* (Browning) – long slog to an old note.
For *soodle* (Clare) – a sidling and slow mooch.
For *quicket* (de la Mare) – fast peepshow of laughing.
For *quoof* (Muldoon) – warm dream-hood in darkening.

Let them catch at a blue moon once in a while
and reach so high across soundwaves crossing
that nothing's to know and knowing's a full
earful of wonder – where sense cuts a caper
with noise, and a nonce-word resounds ever after.

RIDDLING HELL

Riddle me, riddle me ree.
Two men stand up-to-the-knee
stumped in mud or sinking in quicksand
clubbing each other to death, maybe,
in a last deserted no-man's-land.

Here's no answer come to hand.
Here's no question. Try to understand.
Is it I? Is it you? Agree. Disagree.

A MUSICIAN IN WAR TIME

Her hands in mourning
        for peg-nuts, a scroll
F-holes and purfling
        in the wood's hollow
four strings tensed
        to a bridge, open-work
frog and eyelet
        pearling a bow –

for growth-rings of spruce
        formed centuries ago
weatherings of ebony
        compact as bone
for the secret run
        of threads gone viral
the coded mycelium
        of a leaf-mouldered ground.

Her fingers, grief-stricken
        for the fret and lament
of each clear note
        pitched to resound
from belly and ribs
        of a dead thing living
that dares to sing
        so we hear ourselves thinking –

now empty-handed
        her fingers slack
for no music calls
        to console the sorrowful
to restore the forest's
        ancient phoning –
the notes' tall trees
        in our ears, atoning.

BOOK

I cradle it close, not counting how many hours
I've lost in story – my life on hold for the lives
    running along its lines.

I cup its light box, packed and hollow, shiny
to touch and slightly foxed – break cover to find
    fossil prints inside

and hear in the hinge of its spine (winter reeds in the wind)
the thin millefeuilles of its pages whisper and hide
    what they know. Yet consider

how once it was cut from the wooden skin of a tree
that might have shadowed gnats, nightingales, nymphs,
    fungus, weeds,

old fairies in nightshade. I hear it read me, singing
of weathers no one remembers, the planet's trick
    of shaping what lives –

as ancient winters sang in the grain of the wood,
as ice compressed its growth rings, shrank the heart
    for the gift of a Strad.

I am the filament it needs, the dream it conceives,
the expectation that binds: the tree that gives,
    the paper that bears,

the scar that feels. So I, lending an ear
transfer: dead wood, weather, paper, silence
    to a sound in my hands.

PRAYER TO THE SKULL WITH EARS
(votive object in S. Lucilla, Naples)

'Some deformation of the bone,' she explains…
Propped on a shelf

its big-eyed emptiness overlooks
the crumbled jaw

while two auricular knobs, otoliths,
are cocked like a dog's.

Funny friend, were you deaf in life, impaired?
now destined to attend

centuries of prayer in the phone of your head,
your antique landline

earthed in the crypt's dessicating air.
Who are you? Where?

       *

I too beg a hearing (for it's deafness we share)
and whisper once more

into your ears' imaginary receiver,
your squat, chthonic

propensity for dust, yet minded elsewhere:
Can you intercede?

So I call across your dull block of bone,
its mock-moon hollows,

to ask: what's known of us over there?
And do they remember

this ancient atrocity of birth – the horror
of us, in life, at war?

TONE POEM AFTER NEWS

Low
tone
infers
hearing
blink
so…

and aftering
tuneforks
an *oh*
years
ellipses
like stops

a blurry
a funny bone
in ear-phones'
ago in a
for no one
on a bone flute.

News
working
much further
and harder
like near-
or going

soon over
the words
than thinking
its hearing
to far
further

and the brain's
to know
the thing
aloning
unhoming
and further.

Oh
call
no breath
mono-
the ear-
parting

the glottal
bottling
pausing
tone news
drum's thin
me / you

of a bittern's
its no-tune
for the lone
bore-holing
barrier a-
ever aftering.

RETURNS
(Invasion of Ukraine, February 2022)

A February sun amazes the airspace.

(It has happened before. Were we looking away?)

Spring comes round on earth's rotary base.

(I recall toy soldiers in uniform, in rows.)

Today's my birthday. Many happy returns.

(Elsewhere there's shot, mortar shells, grenades.)

A brimstone butterfly lands – a surprise.

(Are they only larking, those boys in the skies?)

And now a tortoiseshell, copper and black.

(A building, shelled, spills a rainbow of lives.)

How count, many happy returns? how sing?

(The wheeze of a bomb starts a count to nothing.)

Listen. There are larks zoning overhead.

(*Granada*'s a pomegranate, likely to bleed.)

From *granatus* – Latin – which is, full of seed.

(Persephone's hunger led to six months in hell.)

I watch green shoots inch out of the ground.

(Crowds in the underground hear sirens, and pray.)

What life can spring from seeds of a grenade?

(It has happened before. We were looking away.)

Happy's a cheer-word, more luck than happening.

(Words are loaded, though they might refrain.)

How many returns, returns, returns?

(*Returning, we hear the larks*. And then a plane...)

THE EMPEROR'S FOOL

—Oh! de moins en moins drôle;
Pierrot sait mal son role?

Jules Laforgue

I

I have clubs, balls, batons, knives,
small party-pieces for a king of fools.
Watch, Daddy. *Catch.* Take your mind off things…

I lift them, spinning – lunaire, solaire –
(mad Pierrot, is it? head-in-the-air).
Here's three-in-one, a magical sum

of nothing, conjured just for the fun –
three, then five, then seven – no win
but to stay alive on your toes, and counting:

six, nine, twelve – cap 'n bells –
(I throw that in to show some learning).
But it's all a toss-up, frolics before the fall,

so *catch!* (my word). Just wish, or wing it.
Where angels play their disappearing tricks
I make a mojo with an arabesque of sticks.

II

So what's the odds, Dad? See, I am
un très méchant fou. Danke, thanks.
That's aptitude in diverse tongues

but don't believe I can tell what is meant.
I shuffle my timed feet, dance my hands,
up-end a hand-stand. No troupes (or troops) –

don't trip now. *Oops!* Double-quick, double-think,
now it's balls in the air. (Who's winning this affair?)
Tanks? (no thanks) – they're a roll to nowhere.

Look now. I toss three balls, catch two,
launch four, then five, stand on one leg.
I'm Pulcinella, that's chicken-and-egg –

little hen, new-hatched from the albumen
of birth and shroud. I'm fooled for wise –
that's one sly innocent for your mock-amen.

III

Watch this, Poppa. My devil-stick whisks
them over and up in showers of falling.
No harm done. Just batons of rain

cheating their base. So I dance, dance
on gravity's own grave, to cadge a laugh,
earn a reprieve, alleviate a living –

no trick more transparent, no cheat more clear.
Open your eyes, Pop. Papochka, listen.
The rhythm repeats with military precision:

beat this, beat this: for liveries, let live,
for marches, malarky, for killers, for kicks.
I smile and slide to a *paso doble*

then juggle my sticks (how many? count quick).
For a pittance I'd play, yet rescue each one
in the grace of its fall, in the face of what's done.

IV

Look, Papa! *Diabolo*, they call it.
I can fetch those flames from the pit of hell,
twit the devil and make him spin

tipped like a top, whirled like a torch
that takes its flame to the rooftop, almost.
No torcher, I. (No torturer, either.)

See how I hatch a diadem of fires.
Stars are sparklers turning a blind eye,
trying not to see the women over there

who will not laugh for all the world.
No joke. Their grief finds no relief
in plate-spinning, flame-throwing shows of words.

Am I you? Are you she? We are who? Who are they?
(Riddle who may, each life's their own).
Shh. It's darkening. Give a toss. Come away.

v

Now for a last, *my pièce de resistance*.
Who'll take a stand? You kill, I riddle.
You mistake, I make: an angel appear

in light reflections from that chamferred steel.
So I, balancing, foozle my short time
(balletic fool), neither resist nor refuse

but waver (*che fece il gran rifiuto*)
one way, then another. Will you spill no tears?
My skill's to keep turning blades in the air.

See here, big Pa, Pappy, Pa-Putin,
I can throw an outline spiked by knives
that will cut no ice, incite no wars

but only glint one moment in the light.
Watch how I magic these knives to nothing.
Can you *see*? No lies, no terror. Just dancing.

RIDDLING VOICES

Voice 1

Therefore, my friend, you must be fooled. Settle for nothing.
A fool's nothing is your only pure gold, a nugget, a jewel

that pays no bills, feeds no mouths. So watch and listen.
Work and wait. This cold's your place to learn a lifelong

loneliness in, for speaking from, or staying with.
Don't rush or fret. Just pay attention. Know that others

will take no note, though notes are all you have to comb
the airways of our shared, breathable intercom.

Voice 2

So what's this thing
that notes its nothing
keeps no promise

leaves no trace
except to repeat
scribble-and-delete?

Voice 3

it is the instant, taut to breaking
it is a whole life, caught in leaving
it is a meaning, flown by making

Voice 4

as soon played as done
as soon heard as lost
as soon here as gone –

a poem forgets
itself to be
read again, and lets

a listening link
connect, so others might
hear themselves think.

SUMMONING HEAVEN

I might apprehend an angel at the night's wide door.
But nothing to speak of there – just a sampler of stars,
a stage-curtain full of holes, ancient and backlit,

or an arras of winks, telling how the joke's on us
who long to imagine an audience, an acoustic hall
with quicklights flashing like calls or an SOS.

This night confutes the colour-spectrum of my sight.
Silence tamps the short hertz-range of my ears.
Yet an angel still waits to come in – called love, or something.

FIRST LOVE

No legs no tail no eyes
a stuffed, furry tube with whiskers –
matched misnomer, homemade patch
    of scraps
but *rat* it was I took to heart, night after night.

So learned that names might figure
as whiskers stand for rat entire –
the lopped body hugged nightlong
    for love
of the thing hidden in a furry wrap: the word in its skin.

IN THE MUSEUM OF THE RUDE ARTS

'he himself asked me what death was', *Iris Origo, of her dying 7-year-old son.*

White and cool
the place, a showcase
for crocks and trinkets
votives, souvenirs
rough-cast accessories
mirrors, goblets

homespun stuff
from earth's old rubble
puzzled together
untouchably near.
Corredo, I read:
that's grave goods or gear

kit for the journey
a ticket to fare
safer through death's
stone-cold corridor –
small keeps for leaving
who knows how far? –

loom weights for yarn
dishes of cracked ware
small pots of perfume
to clear the air
oil lamps to light
the darkness there.

But something runaway
not curated to stay
is unnumbered here.
Is it grief, hunger? –
these crocks all piece-meal
these beads in a heap.

Remember, remember
(is it a party game?)
Such odd things arranged
in this cool glass grave
unused, unhandled
so lonely, saved.

But what stops me dead
is a rude clay doll
articulately limbed
the face erased
by three thousand years
staring at the dark –

a quaint understudy
(clutched to heart maybe
loved to bits)
that asks, and still asks…
lost among the past's
surprising survivals.

No art about it –
unless just the clay's
to mould and earth us
first and last
each faceless face
bound to underground.

Who knows how far?
What kit or ticket?
Some child's weak query
dumbfounds our answer.
So this gawky moppet
beyond belief or story

still calls us out
for truths too hard
lies full of doubt:
sweet dreams, sleep tight.
The child's long gone.
Clay doll, dream on.

OPTICS: FOR WRITING A POEM

At first they're stars – blink and you miss –
peripheral visions encountered in hindsight,
peepshow chancers caught like afterthoughts
of facts lost so many memories ago –
winning glimpses, flashes of distraction.

Then, dead-centre – in a porthole of the void
travelling towards you, hogging the blind spot,
they're jostlers, sticklers, pointless malingerers
summoned to witness there's no vacuum in nature,
just the brain's old longing for what's not there.

So the eye, see, will plant in your blindness,
bang in its bulls'-eye, its macular black,
something you never meant to think or know
that slipped your will and lives without you:
its ghost-light quickens in the line of no sight.

SUGAR POPPET: ALL SOULS' NIGHT

Here's my wee pappy man – will you grow?
This night's a time for company. I pause.
    A cold air sighs.
Come by. Come over. Here's an open window

to show the way any soul might go.
This dream of being's so sweet, yet sad.
    Won't you stop for a bite?
Perhaps I expect no body to show

unless, see here, this forked, akimbo
phantom fattens in the oven's time.
    Will you rise, my mannikin?
my raisin-eyed, light fancy fellow?

I remember – but living seems so long ago.
Will you take time out of your timelessness
    to drop by, break through –
maybe just riff a hand, dip a toe

among us and feel our loneliness, sorrow?
Look, so sweet this cookie look-alike,
    this sugar and almond
impress of a death. Will you rise? Will you grow

my pretty, my mortal poppet? Now, let go
for one night only – and I'll dream we eat
    the sweetmeats of pleasure
together once more. Is that a sigh at the window?

All Souls – In Sicily, on the day of the dead, the custom was to bake
human-shaped cakes, and open the windows to entice the dead
home to share a meal.

CRUCIFORM SONNET ON THE ART

Punctuating nails
heart hammered in
sinews of phrase
stretched to the limit.

(Cross wise wit's no wiser than a frolic in spirit.)

All seems freehand
words' lucky dip
till you cut and pare
a fetish and time it
right to the finish
then chip what's left
to human shape
to make execution
live on the page.

LINES: LINEN

Those rippled stems, retted to ferment
then scutched and heckled, damped and dried,
have threaded the loom's weighted music

since Penelope shuttled her weft and woof:
remember / forget, forget / remember,
a first draft done, delete, start again –

or Eve among the weavers in the sun
teased soft bast into swaddling or shroud –
or the crony Fates measured out, cut down

the thin skin of the living in their hands
to spin a length of time for each
and snip the thread, sooner or late.

Sweet linen, intimate, cool as ancient,
drawn from the flax-fields of the earliest world,
I might touch 30,000 years of wear

feeling this sheet drawn up to my chin:
feel strips of mummy-wrap, paper, canvas,
the long proximities of flesh and grass.

And then remember one I used to know –
who paused between life's facts and story
only as long as it took to fold

(like someone lingering, tidying up,
lost between one world and another)
the blood-soaked linen, three days old –

as if to leave some light human touch
in the precious, suffered, folded stuff
to the women who'd come, and know it for their own.

LAST JUDGEMENT
(Tintoretto, Venice)

Above, a cyclone of souls whooshed through
the Lord's high-speed sorting tumbler,

its central torrent sluiced from on high
to spin the endless current of bodies –

vague lost faces, buttocks and hands
all trumpet-driven one way or another

in a cosmic wash-out, till you might imagine
them rinsed from existence forever and ever.

*

But below, there's still time. Earth holds its own:
bare sluggish shapes that wake to themselves

half-formed, half-known, between two worlds
stirring into flesh, yet cheek by jowl –

is it a plague pit? – and sudden luminous
threads of gold shining at eye height.

Here's a crammed plot, a packed quagmire
of souls hallucinated out of the soil –

*

some nearly whole, like those three women
pausing, watching, considering their ground:

one, half-out of her grave, absorbed,
turns to see two corpses embrace,

another touches her hair – such hair too! –
and rests a hand on some wormy thing

as if she caressed a friend's thigh, to wake
the sleeping dead to love again.

                    *

Theirs might be all the time in the world
beyond the trumpets' rounding alert –

earth's overseers, watchful, unperturbed,
lost in a dream of yearning and reverse,

minding a stray bone, checking a plait
between fact and fable, the muck and the shine.

They seem at home in this new fashioning,
this slow dressing-room before the maelstrom.

                    *

Come again, old echoes – *Can these bones live?*
Here, they pause like there's no forever,

no reckoning overhead – but lost in thought
on the ground's fractured hollows and spills,

rummaging things still piecing together,
puzzled from old disarticulated bits

as if someone gardened nature for a yield
of dreams-come-true among the uprooted weeds.

        *

And still, light catches the glory of their hair,
these dreamy malingerers, ladies of the night.

You'd think the artist had forgotten his theme
and dreamed, with them, of a garden of bones

rising, remembered, all-wondering, unjudged,
beloved and touchable. Who else but he

might trans them lovingly into themselves,
and hold them beautiful, in time, on earth?

EL SOPLON

Ragamuffin boy, flame-charmer, verger of the night.
'*Ohhh*', he pouts, though it's only the wish of a sound
as he tilts the wick of a taper to an embering stick
and cradles a light in the secret reflection of his eyes.

It's dark as pitch all round. Only his face
conceives the magic of a flame the painter needs
to elicit an act of wonder from a dull routine.
The boy's concentrated stare is close, bent down,

holding that dream alive between two hands.
So touchwood might take fire from a rose-tipped splint
to illuminate a thought, expose a crime.
But no one knows what art this art is for.

And still, he'd cajole a creature out of a sigh,
his parted lips a notation, a sound in paint
thrown from the deep shadow-play of light and shade
where a flame might catch its footing, come alive, multiply.

Is it mischief, service, faith? He blows to shine
the mystery of it, honing his breath of life
on night's impenetrable void, Promethean boy!
Who steals the spill might light creation's fire.

El Soplon – El Greco's 'Boy Blowing on a Taper', in the Museo di
Capodimonte, Naples

ASCENSIONS

Pizzofalcone. Capodimonte. L'al di là.
Heavens heave out of our dreams, but sky's the limit.

So many – ascending in faded wind-blown gowns,
their dangled toes tickled by what lies below

yet buoyed on pillows of cirrus or cumulus cloud,
on sunsets flushed underfoot like toeholds of home ground –

so many countless souls surfed on the thermals
of a hope that wafts them upwards just out of reach,

and will give, for the loss of weather, weightiness, world,
a spectator seat in blue air and a halo of gold.

*

And here's the old lift again, heaving up with a jolt:
OTIS. It was Greek to me, a child reading

so as not to hear the sickly cranking wheeze,
the quaking shudder of something coming to life

under my feet at the drop of a five-lire piece –
with its pretty swimming dolphin in a silver sea.

So I'd read, re-read OTIS, for a charm to appease,
holding my breath for fear of my own weight

as the cables groaned and tautened, shivering alongside
till the saving stone's deadweight tipped the balance halfway,

its blank grey slab a blindfold, cutting out the light,
as it headstoned down to earth on its contrary way.

*

Now there's no one to meet me when the lift stops short
of the fifth penultimate floor, missing its threshold.

Nonna, you've long upped and gone, as if at the touch
of that button I never dared press, unnumbered, unnamed,

key to some skylit attic or service room,
some high imaginary entry into emptiness.

But no cloudy ascensions for you, no hustling montages
of souls hauled on the winch and lift of faith,

no airy triumphs flying, foot-off-the ground,
in rowdy hugger-mugger frescoes smudged with age.

I'd wish you just one small dolphin – to take you lightly
across the bay and out. (Now, will five lire pay?)

'PARAÍSO'

I pass it daily now on the homeward stretch –
all that's left of a place: a name, a house,
some brave ill-fated venture making the best

of nowhere's edge of town, some dim-lit diner
rumbled by heavy lorries, now poster-patched,
the door shuttered up for good, no bell for answer.

In the yard a bin's blown over, a syringe on the grass –
ecstasy's empty cartridge has blown its shot.
A rose sheds rosy petals for a sanguine mark.

What's left is just this sadness, damps and draughts
to crack a cheap façade and leach its lettering.
Is it some crooked joker's last good laugh?

Here's heaven's own dump – a keep of what's to save:
loose bin-bags shredded by wind, empty cans thrown in,
the whispered losings, leavings, of the lives we live.

Yet still I read 'Paraíso'… is it haunt or habit?
Memory's hashtag keeps that long lost address
though the foliate rose has shed its gold coronet.

And the orient word sings on, high and weathering.
It sounds a snatch, a riff, a tune cut adrift.
Is this what's left of hope? No less than everything.

IN THE ROPE-MAKERS' YARD

Those who know the ropes know twine's
a strength, a keckling bind – mankind's
own bearing, twisted uprightness,
a thing reflexed from mixed designs.

We're trussed to helix turns, drawn double,
stressed to ourselves by make and choice.
I hold this thing a scourge, a tether –
old rope? But *skip*. Now it's miracle, rubble.

REMEMBERING GARDENS

Each step's a knock
on lapidary
ways of rock

on things dismissed
to wishing wells
or burial kist

so earth might let
us live, to begin
to dream, to forget

The beck, here and there, runs brick-red. A rubric of pawprints on the cinder track shows where a dog, all clarty with mud, took a bitter drink – then bolted and swerved into a belt of heather. Those stencil marks won't wash away quickly, though they fade as they go... a forensic tease. Ochres and rusts are colours that linger, like something you know under the skin, as if earth's secret haemoglobin might enliven a ditch. Its dull red seeps into tarns and pools, deepens the shade of campion or ling, flushes the iron grey stone in patches. You're reminded of it in the rust-fretted bars of an unhinged gate that's fallen sideways and makes no closure, holds nothing in. Yet its punctured, broken, hollow rods can turn the wind to a phantom, singing.

This land was once threaded with rifts of ore, rich for the picking. Magnetic ironstone, the geologists called it, and fast on their tracks came surveyors and speculators, leasers and buyers, drivers and miners. In the space of two decades, from the 1860s to the 1880s, a rural backwater of two hundred people was turned into a busy industrial hub, worked by five thousand. In spite of deep gullies and awkward gradients, the remote moorland was quickly connected by rail and incline to the main routes north: to Ingleby and Middlesbrough, and on to the Durham coalfields. Wagons, called 'tubs', engine sheds and bunkers, haulage wheels and loading hoppers pockmarked the view, as the new industrial power of steam was brought to the unaccommodating landscape, to extract wealth from its ground. Now, only curious walkers pause – in the quiet that has buried so much noise. The hills have healed, covering their scars with bracken and heather, smoothing their dumps of calcine dust, concealing entries to drifts and shafts, air vents and wells. A hopeful cover of vegetation now softens the raw stone, once unearthed by so much force. Only here and there, like the memory of something live and hurt, that old dull stain still leaches out, discolouring the neutral element of water in strangely wounded pools or tarns.

Walking along the contour of the hill, you follow the old route of the railway. The path is wide and the going, easy. This is no picturesque scene of peaks and hollows, but a plain canvas of horizontal straight lines drawn by a few simple brush strokes. Above, the heather is brown and bare under the sky – a knotty tangle of black roots and stems, till late July blesses it with flowers; below, there's bracken and the dry-stone walls start, brokenly, forgetfully, containing lost pastures, rough set-asides; and finally in the valley, where the soil is a little deeper, a little more workable, there's a pastoral scene of fields and trees, farmsteads and barns. An eye might sweep over it all in a moment and get the picture. But turn a corner along the flank of the hill, and you find surprising industrial landmarks: the topless tower of a stone chimney, the regular arches of a row of kilns – Roman, in their look of age-old purpose – then more kilns, square constructions built into the hillside, their great herring-boned blocks of stone lined by firebricks still faintly rouged by the heat they contained. There's a terrace of ruined cottages and, ahead, the gable-end of what were called the Black Houses – dwellings once tarred with bitumen against the weather. All that's left of them is one square aperture looking out across the dale – a folly, it might seem, or a primitive camera for taking the view. Its sculpture frames the slow curve of the valley, bringing what is there into casual focus.

What is it about landscape? I've returned to this place for more than thirty years, driven by some need for its quiet, the calming indifference of its hills – or perhaps by that instinctive animal hefting that learns, at some level, to return to base. Like the sheep who keep to their allotted terrains, I have gravitated back in a kind of homing. Returns, after all, are the natural way of things, seasonal or yearly, living and dying. What comes round will round again, following the impersonal clock of the planets. So spring, after the long silence of winter, brings the dale to life in sounds once more. A mild January day sends a lark half-heartedly chattering skykwards. Late February, and the first tentative migrants arrive: curlews heading inland to nest, their faint *cue, cue,* like a note with nowhere to go, a hopeless tuning repeat, and no tune. But a week or so later it has grown into a flutey, bubbling call, a prolonged coloratura climaxing at each stop. Soon the curlews are joined by lapwings, their slender crested gait, stalking or watching, become a clownish tumbling dance, all flapping wings and whoops and squeals, as the male performs his courtship ritual often late into the night. Snipe might sometimes be heard on a still night, high up and invisible, their tail-feathers playing an eerie xylophone – quick scales of notes travelling up and down as they drum the air through which they fall. In late March the first wheatears arrive. They chit and tut, bobbing defiantly on a moorland stone, then flying, white-arsed, always just a little beyond reach. Late April, the cuckoo starts its routine plainchant of minor thirds in the valley below – an echoing repeat that resonates confusingly, as if a decoy disguised its whereabouts. And finally, those three far-flown birds of summer: martins, dipping and chattering along the roadside in search of wet mud for their lintel nests; swallows, with their fantastic appliqué of turns as they swoop and twitter, bursting with news; and lastly, in late May, the high tragic swifts, their chorus of screams underscoring, like a relentless alarm, the whole bright order of summer.

Returns fit the order of things in this place. They mark the year-in, year-out rounding of the planet, while offering a kind of rough consolation for what's lost on the way. For this is also a landscape of no-return, carrying the cost of its human history visibly on its surface – a cost that speaks in silent ruins, where the engine of wealth took its toll of lives. Injured, they died, crushed by wagons, caught by explosives, stunned by falling stones – died often lucklessly, of gangrene, tetanus, septicaemia: a boy named John Hugill, twelve years of age, crushed to death between two tubs of ironstone he was hitching for the incline; a man named John Wilcocks, killed inside the mine by a sudden fall of stones; another, Thomas Harwick, completely buried under a collapse of shale; and another, George Kay, slightly injured by a stone falling on his leg, who died nine days later when gangrene set in; then another, and another... What is left of that history still tells on these hills, though the lists of names have largely disappeared except from the records of local history.

And so it happens that a ravaged landscape might become protected heritage; a sad eyesore, a national monument. The lines between them are thin as the grass that hides a railroad and makes a walkers' right of way. What remains of those mines, kilns and chimneys is now protected from the elements, fenced off from passers-by, explained and dated in the tourist brochures, though like all standing stones they also look like something's tombstone. A hundred years on we admire the masonry, the weighted symmetries of those hewn blocks, the fine ingenuity of a balanced arch that has survived abandonment, theft and weather. Now the place offers a rest cure for the stressed. *So peaceful*, we might say, dreaming in our own tongues. Our monoglot imaginations can readily ignore the panic of a lamb on the wrong side of a fence, the nightlong wail of ewes first deprived of their young, the miniature scream of a hunted mouse, and all the tiny insect palavers, half out of earshot, through which we pass. Only sometimes, perhaps woken in the night by the sudden screech of a barn owl, we might start to hear, in the sounds of nature, our own imaginations cry out loud.

Returning to these hills, as I do, to walk, daydream, to sleep with the sounds of owls and pheasants, lambs and ewes, is, I know, a luxury of the city dweller for whom the landscape needs neither working nor minding, but is a fair-weather option. Yet sometimes, walking along the railway path, levelled for the traction of those injuring tubs, heavy with spoils, it's hard to forget the underlying story of this quiet, self-absenting escape. Something lurks not far under the national park's tidied footpaths and waymarked routes. It's as if, walking, you might still hear the ratchet repeat of wagon wheels, smell the discharge of coal and steam, catch the calcine dust in your lungs. Or as if you might feel, among the underlying quicks of grass everywhere, those recurrent tumuli of the man-made: the shadows of sleepers, originals long removed, whose underlay can be felt like the alternation of something soft then hard, smooth then raised, under your feet. Unquiet sleepers, in the stepping imaginations of the living, might still shift close by, restless underground.

LARK RISE

Funny little wind-up soul –
your coil-spring ascension's a call
to daylight, alarming and comical.

As if you were climbing a rope
of notes, your wittering treble
heli-resurrects to a high middle-

distance on a fluster of wings –
a chaffering gizmo to riddle
the quiet's uncertain interval.

This mimic rendition of a round-up
reel's as long as it's singable,
as high as it's hung on invisible

threads, like some winching elastic
stretched till it pings, and you tumble
to begin again, begin again: no trouble.

CURLEW

So early?   comer

        turning   a curlicue   cut

to   *cue*   *cue*

        in a moor's   mist   in the barely   lit

February   daylight

        in an early world   of beginners   beginning

the art of false   starts

                master   imparter.

(Listen, poet)

                                        starting's

        the hardest

                call   before a roll

coo–eee   *coo–eee–u*

        a haunted   yodel

                stopping   short

like spring's initial   longing   and pause

                imponderable   rigmarole.

CANENS TO PICUS

Spring brings a bird back, knocking at my heart –
drummer-boy, gold-badged, stickler for a touch
now tapping for heartwood, figuring rough bark,
nit-picking, piquant, my Picus, my love.

Circe's changeling, now hamstrung in claws,
handcuffed in wings, you must rap to enter.
That heckling drill batters my ear,
a hammer-blow still percussing the air.

You're too high to reach, too other, too flighty.
You cannot tune me to your dummy key.
I cannot keep you human, answering,
Picus, my heartbeat, my pulse-stopping beauty.

Sweet bird-boy patched in scarlet and gold,
your coded rhythm's too fast to read.
Your beak can't kiss, only frets and bores
the wood for echoes of yourself instead.

Once I could stop the rivers in their flow,
move stones and trees to listen closer.
Now Tiber drains the marrow from my bones,
filches my song's heart-blood for water.

And I am only my own absence, found –
a *singing* entered, light as air,
some Orphic girl, no name but a tune
in a book somewhere – I am melody's own ear.

The nymph Canens (singing) could sing like Orpheus, but through
the jealousy of Circe, her beloved boy, Picus, was turned into a
woodpecker. Canens, in despair, threw herself into the Tiber.

MURMURATIONS

Dusk draws them in   to net or sieve
  the light's paling   at close of day

  wingtip-to-tip   a fluvial knit
    of starlings gather   feathering together

    in thousands, tens of   thousands, a spill
      of shapes that mimic   a giant brain thinking.

      Una passeggiata   *paesaggio, saggio* –
      no destination   just the ins and outs

      of blank air tethered   by a fretwork of nerves
      a willing, perfect   intricacy of wills.

    Who knows why it is?   knotting the last light
    in ropes of flight   then inverting, dispersing

  as if a script were   writing in their wings
  à la piste, pointilliste   through spaces of sky.

                    *

So I pause to see
Ponte Sisto.

how near, how far.
Siste, viator.

Stay, traveller,
to lock and loosen –

another flock starts
an instagram

of moving parts
a net, a trawl

like, very like
a cloud, a camel.

What makes this shape?
to switchback, split

Which bird decides
re-constellate

then dive out of sight
a charcoal storm cloud?

and crosshatch into
Birds of a feather

no one knows why
their shadow crosses

(gone tomorrow)
this bridge where we

linger to remember
and read a sound

auguries of flight
in the murmur of a shape.

A CHILD IN THE GARDEN

She takes her pick, a yellow, a pink,
their bright corollas tendered in a glass –
a pretty killing, perhaps an offering?

as if she culled the colours of the world
and held them light under the midday sun –
a floret sundae, horn of plenty.

Young Flora, Pandora – how soon her cup
overflows in dead-heads. So she tips it up
and spills a still-life on the garden path.

Alas, my part's not to save the flowers
or praise the art – but to grieve and laugh
for the human child who can cut their hearts.

TWO SONGS

1 ALLOTMENT

Here's all it is:
mulch and mineral
sun and rain
for braided greens
spinach everlasting.

I know my place
patrol the perimeter
permit no entry
to a ground as narrow
or wide as a world –

a ground that's open
to skies, fenced in
my portion of planet
a lease of clods
for mucking in.

I've hung these toggled
tomatoes on a string
hooked my runners
where celeriac's all
a root-ball of worms.

Green butts and bins
demarcate my demesne
my strength and heft
a dedication
to compostible waste.

I work and work
my plot, my one place –
nursery to grave.
Next door's all to seed
in a scatter-song of weed.

2 A SCATTERING

Neither sown nor reaped
                no work but dream
                                no rule but waste

I stand and stare
                wits to the wind
                                given to anywhere's

patch of ashes
                weeds and tares
                                (small yield of words)

as if the heart's
                screaming-meemie
                                running amok

were footing the green
                careening the garden
                                clod-hopping the clay

to spoil the crop
        of gathered-in meaning
                till I think no more –

facing the end
        for which we begin
                our conclusions carried

the length of living
        to grief and leaving
                death and missing –

yet snatch a song-line:
        the barley mow
                for each new rising

and watch my earth
        take what remains
                in waste and scattering.

A SECRET GARDEN

Whose are these
>glinting scarers twirled on threads?
>circling compacts coloured by a world's

mirrored palette
>its multitudinous shades of rainbow
>thrown by the wedging cut of a prism?

Who has hung
>these silver wheels like cymbals meant
>to flash and spread a spectrum in the sun?

Just old CDs
>someone has set to scare the birds
>among the plums and figs and pears

to shiver and wink
>and catch distractions on a cadmium screen
>that tags the green mortality of leaves.

These razor-thin
>flashes of brightwork turn in the wind
>mimic-mirrors of the nature of things.

What brings me here
>to a twinkling orchard hung with ware
>nature fruiting like a Christmas fair

as if the graft
>of slow generation from bud to rot
>were helped by toys, or is it art? –

by an installation

        of moons or else a constellation?
        I watch them turn like memory's hum.

On air each earring

        twitched, might make a hearing visible.
        In sun-shot grooves their lost music sings.

LOWNA QUAKER GRAVEYARD

Queer names: *horsetails* – growing by a stream,
their fleshy thumbs-up among the hellebores

and old as the first life-forms, stem-jointed.
We might be seeing the earth without us,

still and silent – with just these rude pink
peeping Toms from the nether regions.

Then we found its roofless boundaries:
four stone walls circumscribing a square,

a perfect enclosure with nothing to show
for the hundred and more lying mulched below.

*

No names, no dates – as if pure form
contained forgetting just to hold it there,

where so many uncleared centuries of leaves
made all the sense our feet could read

from a scrabble of bones lightly whispered over,
the last vestiges of what might be believed.

Not even a clearing, no set-aside space
marked theirs and ours, just trees either side

that rooted clean through those dark dormitories
where something, once, gave up its name.

Come in. Take cover. This sun might burn to the bone.
Here's shade, darkness at noon, a fluted cavern,
its aerial roots like bell-pulls, sallies – cords
for corralling a troll (bring bell, book and candle),
for calling: Rapunzel, Rapunzel, let down your hair,
for tolling a death-knell (who goes there? where?).
They fall in ropes and probes like wooden rain.

Come further in. Now listen. It seems a silence.
But pull out the stops to hear this panelled room
where a voluntary of downpipes sounds their names:
Tibia, Cor de Nuit, Vox Humana.
Who'll expiate, in lyrical turns and phrases,
the brain's lunatic stake in forms of words?
in pilliwinks, prisons, the logic of smoke and faith?

Observe the yawning arch of this ribbed vaulting,
shady, cool as a church, a hub of repose
that crypts the ash of heretics earthed below.
Then touch these living cables, neural roots
still nosing, nosing... going where no one knows.
Dry blades of grass, cat's-whiskers, shiver as we pass.
What human voices are chambered in this live cave?

Whatever was gardened here must now compose
the green coping of a tree, its girth and age –
and all the music made or scriptures sung
in frames to make what's beautiful forget:
the cry that hurt the note, the scream that prayed,
the scaffold in the wood, burnt ash at base –
and how fine words might frame a shade for graves.

Piazza Marina, Palermo – where heretics were burned at the stake
by the Spanish Inquisition.

CALENDULA SICULA
(i.m. Kevin Jackson)

Chaff, I think, and shuffle a pack of dormant stuff
won from forgotten depositions, centuries of death,
in chalk and limestone – barely, see? an advance on dust –
discovered in a drawer like a lost love-letter, this comfortless Easter.

I read its faded envelope again: Pantalica, 07,
and think how gardens flower about the dead in rented sepulchres.

Sicilian marigolds, earthy aureoles, reaped from the cliffside's
plundered tombs, a future countdown in survival's calendar –
this cold Good Friday of a year of deaths, I recall them flourishing
in buttonholes of bone, bonny in the sunlight's open prospect.

From buried dust, a corolla of gold – like Mary in marigold.
From earth's dumb stone – an anthem chanted in chrysanthemum.

IMPOSTER

Who is this creep, this ancient misfit?
She hangs on me like a pauper relative,
pulls a face to greet my disbelief,
wrinkles her nose at my guarded self-regard.

Who does she think she is, this hag?
fingering my hands with her gnarled digits,
feeling my pulse, distressing my skin,
putting that look of fear into my eyes.

Each morning she's there in the frame, reflecting.
How did she get in, with her pouchy bags,
face-mask for a face? By what black art
will she twist my arm to extrapolate a heart?

BARGAIN BASEMENT

Old curiosities, odds 'n ends
        (some yesterday or centuries ago)
ends, mostly – loose or met –
        and no odds-on to win, all shelved

as I remember, I remember
        (still that line from somebody's poem)
words to conjure for a name or face,
        job-lots of phrases, hand-me-downs

for all the minutes suffered to live
        in this nerve-kit of my altering skin –
things forgotten in the knockdown room
        of life's necessary unremembering:

a terror, a toy, a doll's corpse stare,
        a biped A in the flutter of a first book,
a loved lost name, a promise not kept,
        all tabbed by the brain's *delete* by default.

So accept from birth: forgetting's what we know –
        those wind-blown hoardings for an empty shop –
my tongue too slow to log how it went.
        Love? Forget it. *All must go.*

TO THE LORD OF FORGETTING

that I may not remember duration
that days might slip out of mind
even weeks, months, years
that I may not hold every moment's live
sensation in mind or try to memorise
    every conversation

that I may recall my fleeing self
only in selective reinvention
and then recall it less and less
as the kind lord of forgetfulness
eases a way out to a clearing
    even from myself.

CYCLAMEN AT THE WINTER SOLSTICE

Something... I forget –
        something the brain hunts backstairs for
in cobwebby haunts,
        a neural cubby-hole that has shut its door.

I'm offguard, distracted
        by this arabesque of fans, a pinwheel turn-around
(which flipside's right?)
        flunkey to the cold moon, pearl on the ground,

yet winging it, very still –
        flung from a whirlwind into this world,
thin wrapper, litter,
        love-letter sugar-spun, a whiteness unfurled.

Yet something... I forget –
        standing waylaid by this light-flare dancer,
icy marker
        of a dark path growing longer and harder –

by a grace so utterly
        careless, other, so obliviously keen
that I stand accused
        of being here, still needing to explain.

Dear winter survivor –
        (how many now dying?) I might live to know
forgetting's a life gift.
        I came for something... Is it time to go?

ACKNOWLEDGEMENTS

Huge thanks to friends and colleagues, poets and non-poets, who at various stages read all or some of these poems, and offered thoughts, comments, changes – especially John Kerrigan, Harriet Marland, Stav Poleg and Claire Preston, but also Mona Arshi, Emily Gowers, Robin Holloway, Robert Leighton and Adrian Poole.

Michael Schmidt has been a constant source of encouragement over the years, while John McAuliffe's sharp, editorial eye and ear were exactly what I needed at the end. He saw the shape of this volume almost before I could see it myself. To all at Carcanet, my heartfelt thanks.

I am also grateful to the editors of the following journals in which earlier versions of these poems appeared:

Archipelago for 'Stone Prayer' and 'Unquiet Sleepers'

The Dark Horse for 'Paraíso'

London Magazine for 'Sea Level' and 'Pebbles'

The New Yorker for 'Water like a Stone'

PN Review for 'Tarn and Wall', 'Ditty for the Poets', 'Calendula Sicula', 'Cyclamen at the Winter Solstice' and 'From the Lighthouse'

Stand for 'Lines / Linen', 'In the Museum of the Rude Arts', 'Allotment' and 'Cruciform Sonnet on the Art'

Think: A Journal of Poetry, Fiction, and Essays, for 'Fish Market' and 'Bargain Basement'

TLS for 'By the Tide of Humber' and 'Lark Rise'

'By the Tide of Humber' was commissioned for *Companions of his Thoughts More Green: Poems for Andrew Marvell*, ed. David Wheatley, Broken Sleep Books, 2022.

'Returns' was published in *A Festschrift for Maurice Rutherford*, ed John Lucas, Shoestring Press, 2022.